THE MERMAID

Adapted from
Hans Christian Andersen's The Little Mermaid

by

Cassandra Fumi

CURRENCY PRESS
The performing arts publisher

⊕ LA MAMA

CURRENT THEATRE SERIES

First published in 2021
by Currency Press Pty Ltd,
PO Box 2287, Strawberry Hills, NSW, 2012, Australia
enquiries@currency.com.au
www.currency.com.au

in association with La Mama Theatre Company Melbourne

Typeset by Dean Nottle for Currency Press.
Cover features Allegra Di Lallo; photo by Caspar Plum.
Cover design by Katy Wall for Currency Press.

Currency Press acknowledges the Traditional Owners of the Country on which
we live and work. We pay our respects to all Aboriginal and Torres Strait
Islander Elders, past and present.

A catalogue record for this
book is available from the
NATIONAL
LIBRARY   National Library of Australia
OF AUSTRALIA

Contents

THE MERMAID

    Prologue: The Classroom   1

ACT ONE: SEA   3

    Scene 1: Creation
    Scene 2: People And Not People
    Scene 3: Sun Garden
    Scene 4: A Saviour
    Scene 5: Past The Stars
    Scene 6: Above
    Scene 7: Sea Scat
    Scene 8: The Sea Witch and Her Polypi

ACT TWO: LAND   12

    Scene 9: Transformation
    Scene 10: No Prince Home
    Scene 11: The Stories We Tell
    Scene 12: Duck, Duck, Goose

ACT THREE: AIR   18

    Scene 13: Sonic Waves
    Scene 14: The Release
    Scene 15: Fifteen

HANS CHRISTIAN ANDERSEN'S
THE LITTLE MERMAID   21

Theatre program at the end of the playtext

A NOTE ON THE TEXT

This is a contemporary performance text in response to Hans Christian Andersen's fairytale, *The Little Mermaid.*

This work blends aspects of both tragic and comic forms to retell the narrative. In this adaptation, spoken text is interwoven with movement sequences to explore the story.

A great adventure. A coming of age. An epic journey of self-actualisation and finding voice.

AUTHOR'S NOTE

The Mermaid is a devised piece of contemporary performance, a reimagining and reclamation of Hans Christian Andersen's *The Little Mermaid*, based on the collaborative retelling by teenagers and adults. The creative development with Melbourne-based teenagers involved a combination of research, story sharing and physical improvisation where the ideas were brainstormed, clarified and refined through practical experimentation, then scripted, rehearsed and performed. Their interpretations of the story and its surrounding mythology and iconography create the basis for the show.

The performance text operates on two key levels—in terms of language, it splits the written text between the voice of the young mermaid and her older selves using a blend of source texts, such as Hans Christian Andersen's *The Little Mermaid*, poems, pop culture references and verbatim text from teen creators. It further contrasts this with the presence of the all-knowing teenage chorus who create a physical language and image-based score which provides contemporary commentary that counterpoints the behaviour and ideas present in the original text. The chorus may speak as one individual being or as five individual voices at any point in the script.

We are excited by the uniqueness that young people bring to the stage, as performers, and as inheritors of our contemporary myths, beliefs and social structures. Our production draws upon this energy to create a highly visual, sensory and powerful experience for the audience. It is poetic, chaotic, mythical and contemporary all at once. It learns from the past but moves towards a new mythology that draws from traditional character archetypes and folds them into complex, contradictory and authentic human beings.

Cassandra Fumi

The Mermaid was first produced at La Mama Courthouse Theatre, Melbourne, on 14 July 2021, devised and performed by the following cast:

MERMAID 1   Allegra Di Lallo

CHORUS and other roles:

Theo Boltman, An Dang, Allegra Di Lallo, Flora Feldman, Emily Goddard, Mila Jennings, Margaret Mills, Marshall Morgan, Casper Plum, Asha Sheppard, Ella Simons and Frankie Wilcox.

Co-creator and Director, Cassandra Fumi
Artistic Associate, Tennessee Mynott-Rudland
Dramaturgy, Vidya Rajan
Performance Text, Izzy Roberts Orr
Composer, Chrisopher Bolton with Ivy Lou
Set and Costume Designer, Dann Barber
Lighting Designer, Rachel Burke
Assistant Director, Tove Due
Assistant Stage Manager, Holly Anderson
Youth Coordinator, Fiona Spitzkowsky
Images by Casper Plum

CHARACTERS

The character of the Mermaid is played in three iterations by three performers at different stages of life, indicated in the text as:

MERMAID 1, the teenage mermaid protagonist
MERMAID 2
MERMAID 3

The CHORUS is played by five teenagers. They may speak as a collective or as five individual voices at any point in the script. Chorus members take on teh role of auxiliary characters, narrators or themselves. They play the following characters:

SEBASTIAN THE CRAB
A SCHOOL OF FISH
POLYPI, half animal, half plant creatures
THE PRINCE
THE MERMAID'S GRANDMOTHER
THE MERMAID'S FIVE SISTERS
THEMSELVES
A CHILD MERMAID

SETTING

Prologue: A classroom
Act 1: Sea
Act 2: Land
Act 3: Air

Time in *The Mermaid* is mythical and cyclical, and so blends specific time references in and out of each other. Time here is different from historical time. The events that take place 'once upon a time' are recreated here in order to reactivate their force. As it was manifested then so it is becoming now.

This play went to press before the end of rehearsals and may differ from the play as performed.

PROLOGUE: THE CLASSROOM

As the audience enter, a group of teenagers (the CHORUS*) prepare for their dance with their backs to the audience.* SEBASTIAN THE CRAB *is giving a class presentation on the Coney Island Mermaid Parade.*

SEBASTIAN THE CRAB: Are we ready to begin?

Coney Island. The set location for the 1990's hit film *Uptown Girls* starring Dakota Fanning. Dakota Fanning, the sister of young actor Elle Fanning. Elle Fanning, the co-star of Nicole Kidman in the 2017 hit film *The Beguiled*. Directed by Sofia Coppola which got 77% on Rotten Tomatoes. Sofia Coppola, with Warner Brothers, planned to direct and produce an adaptation of *The Little Mermaid*. It got cancelled. Shame. This was going to be a show about mermaid pride. Where else do you see mermaid pride? Coney Island!

Every year 800,000 people hold a mermaid pride parade where you can be proud of yourself and embrace everyone. LGBTQIA+, different races, cultures and everything in between. Where you don't have to be shameful.

Because of poems like this: 'What shall we do with a drunken sailor'.

He reads the poem.

> What shall we do with a drunken sailor
> What shall we do with a drunken sailor
> What shall we do with a drunken sailor
> Early in the morning.
> Hooray! and up she rises
> Hooray! and up she rises
> Hooray! and up she rises
> Early in the morning.

You know where we find drunken sailors? *The Little Mermaid.* It's a shame that the sailors are drunk and agro. But, with the mermaid parade of Coney Island, we can find a place where everyone is embraced and we don't have those silly old drunken sailors. One of my favourite mermaid books is *Julian Is A Mermaid* which talks about a young boy learning about life through mermaids and pride and the LGBT community. We learn more about ourselves. I learn about myself. So join Coney Island pride today. For the mermaids. And for Sofia Coppola and her unmade mermaid film.

People may think princes exist and mermaids don't, but you and I know it is the exact opposite.

Princes don't exist and mermaids, most certainly do.

…

Thank you.

The TEENAGERS *run out dance to the opening theme song from 'H20: Just Add Water'.*[1] *They are all wearing Ariel wigs.*

ACT ONE: SEA

SCENE 1: CREATION

Static white noise increases and decreases in volume until it becomes the sound of crashing waves. MERMAID 1 *sinks into a sea of fabric covered in flowers (her tail). She emerges in the centre of the space, waiting for something to happen, looking up at a central circle of light.*

The CHORUS *put on masks and become completely unified in movement and voice, as a school of fish in murmuration.*

A physical movement score follows, during which the CHORUS *foreshadows the story to come. While they do so,* MERMAID 1 *plants a weeping willow and watches it grow. She arranges her garden to look like the sun.*

Time [CHORUS *check an invisible watch.*]
Storm [CHORUS *brush their hair with an invisible brush.*]
Warning [CHORUS *form a chain behind* MERMAID 1 *three times.*]
Time [CHORUS *check their watches again.*]
Boat [CHORUS *stand in a circle looking up.*]
Saving [CHORUS *raise their arms three times.*]
Meeting Sea Witch [CHORUS *orbit around* MERMAID 1.]
Warning [CHORUS *repeat the touching of* MERMAID 1.]
Potion [CHORUS *drink.*]
Loss of voice [CHORUS *pull their voices out five times.*]
New Legs [CHORUS *jump.*]
Dance [CHORUS *dance with uncertain legs.*]
Statue Longing [CHORUS *cool their feet.*]
Choice [CHORUS *look side to side.*]
Release [CHORUS *stand.*]

> *The* CHORUS *circle around* MERMAID 1, *checking the time.*

> *A* CHORUS *member brings out an angler fish as a birthday cake.*

> *The whole* CHORUS *clap 15 times, in honour of* MERMAID 1's *fifteenth birthday.*

MERMAID 1 *blows out the light on the antenna of the angler fish.*
Silence.

At this point, MERMAID 2 *and* MERMAID 3 *emerge from two seas of fabric covered in flowers (their tails) and blow out an angler fish's light at the same time.*

SCENE 2: PEOPLE AND NOT PEOPLE

MERMAID 2: Before sea or land
　　Before even night
MERMAID 3: Nature wore one mask, since, called chaos.
MERMAID 1: Far out, in the wide sea, the water is blue.
MERMAID 2: Blue as a cornflower. Clear. Clear as the purest crystal.

　　CHORUS *become shells that open and close as if the water flows over them.*

MERMAID 3: It is very, very deep, so deep that if many willows were piled on top of one another they would not reach from the bed of the sea to the surface of the world.
MERMAID 1: Fishes both large and small, glide between the plants,
MERMAID 2: as birds fly among the trees here on land.
MERMAID 1: Living flowers grow out of walls.
MERMAID 3: In the deepest spot of all,
MERMAID 2: stands the castle of the Sea King …

　　MERMAID 1, MERMAID 2 *and* MERMAID 3 *all see the Sea King's castle on the horizon.*

… with walls built of coral and a roof formed of shells, that open and close as the water flows over them.
MERMAID 3: Over everything lies a peculiar flickering radiance as if surrounded by the Air above.

SCENE 3: SUN GARDEN

MERMAID 1 *sings to herself and arranges her garden to look like the sun. The* CHORUS *become her five* SISTERS *and hum to a different tune in their own garden plots.* MERMAID 1 *finds a gold shoe in a shipwreck and plays with it, fascinated.*

MERMAID 1: I can see you, can you see me?
　　Someone will remember us
　　In the future.

She sings some more.

My grandmother told me that out in the upper world, there is something called a sun. A big, burning round thing that makes everything grow and bloom and shine. I asked her, 'Is it like a pearl then?' And she said, 'No, not like a pearl.' So I asked, 'Is it like a sea urchin? Or a shell, or a jellyfish, or a stone?' To all of these things, she said, 'No. No child, the sun is not like anything else in the deep—or anything much at all anywhere. The sun is just the sun, and it is like nothing else.'

The closest thing I can imagine it to be is like when the light comes down through the deep and catches in currents, or splays out dappled all over the ocean floor, making round shapes on the sandscapes. The sun lights everything up, even all the way down here, and so my garden grows. What delicious fruits, what luscious flowers must they have up there, in the upper world? Soon, I will be fifteen—and then I will know.

I dreamed I was carried away on the crest of a wave, up, up into the world above. I watch my face in the mirror of the sea, sun bursting over my back and diving into and over the ocean. The suck of air between my teeth, in my lungs—salt spray and the waves coming, always the waves and sea foam.

I am ready to see a horizon—I want to know what the shore feels like, have the sun on my skin and hear what it's like to speak more than brine and bubbles.[2]

CHORUS: At fifteen, the mermaids come up to the surface of the world.

MERMAID 2: The first went up, voices of human beings, sound of music, noise of carriages and machines.

　　The second went up, a sunset, a flock of swans fly against rose-coloured clouds.

　　The third, a palace and castle amongst trees, a pet dog.

　　Fourth, ships, sky above like a sheet of glass groaning under weight.

　　Fifth, large icebergs, each like a pearl but larger and loftier. Blue lightning darting and flashing back into the sea.

MERMAIDS 1, 2 and 3: [*together*] I go up.

> MERMAID 1 *stands and looks up. The* CHORUS *move as if they have small internal storms in their bellies.*

CHORUS: [*repeating*] By cowardice or courage we are back at this scene.[3]

MERMAIDS 2 and 3: [*together*] By cowardice or courage we are back at this scene. By cowardice or courage we are back at this scene…

> *A movement sequence follows:* CHORUS *begin to walk towards* MERMAID 1, *forcing her forward.*

> MERMAID 2 *and* MERMAID 3 *begin to panic.*

> MERMAID 2 *and* MERMAID 3 *try and stop* MERMAID 1 *from walking.*

> MERMAID 1 *reaches the centre of the stage.*

> *The* CHORUS *form a line at the back of the space and become a horizon.*

> MERMAID 2 *and* MERMAID 3 *accept that the scene has already begun.*

SCENE 4: A SAVIOUR

A boat appears above the stage. It is the Prince's 15th birthday.

Two CHORUS MEMBERS *stand upstage facing each other as if on the boat. One (the* PRINCE*) wears a gold party hat. The other claps fifteen times. They both dance, then toss around the hat like dude bros.[4] The remaining* CHORUS *become the eye of a storm that slowly intensifies.*

The PRINCE *falls into the water and starts to drown.* MERMAID 1 *saves the* PRINCE.

CHORUS: Crushing drowning and burning
CHORUS: Neptune tides
CHORUS: Neptune tides

> *The party hat falls from the* PRINCE. MERMAID 1 *picks it up.*

> *The* PRINCE *doesn't see* MERMAID 1, *who sits on the rocks, clutching his gold hat. He walks off stage.*

Time passes.

CHORUS: In the morning the storm
CHORUS: Had
CHORUS: Ceased; but of the ship
CHORUS: Not a single fragment
CHORUS: Could be seen.

SCENE 5: PAST THE STARS

A member of the CHORUS *becomes the mermaid's* GRANDMOTHER.

MERMAID 1: If men don't drown, do they live forever?

GRANDMOTHER: No, they die too, and quicker than us. We live for 300 years and then become foam on the water. Our souls die and become the seaweed, which, once cut down, ceases to exist. In the upper world they have created a soul which lives forever. After their bodies become dust, they rise through the clear air, up through the thin air, and out past the stars.

MERMAID 1: Why does my soul die? I would give up my 300 years in the sea to be a human if my soul could live forever. I will not become seaweed.

GRANDMOTHER: You can't think about that, you mustn't. We are better off here, everything is better, down where it's wetter, take it from me.

MERMAID 1: There must be something I can do.

GRANDMOTHER: No. Well, only if a human being loved you, as they love themselves, but this has barely happened in the history of the upper world. Only then, would you share their soul and your head would ring with the love of the stars. But I know about what they do for pleasure. And look. Look at your fish tail. Here it is beautiful and essential, and in the upper world it is hideous. To be pretty there you must have legs which can stand, and walk, and run, and open.

Let us be happy here, during our 300 years of life, surely that is enough.

A horn blows from the upper world.

SCENE 6: ABOVE

The CHORUS *walk in with big legs, wearing gold shoes. A surreal movement and text sequence follows.* MERMAID 1, MERMAID 2 *and* MERMAID 3 *walk in corridors up and down stage.*

MERMAID 1: Above.

MERMAID 2: Above.

MERMAID 3: Above.

MERMAID 1: If everything I touch passes into water, the crab scuttling into the cave, the giant squid fighting the whale, each of them dissolving into water…

MERMAID 2: The fish have their schools, the waves have their sets that lash the sand in tandem, the orca have their hunting squads, and me, here…

MERMAID 3: Am I looked upon by the surface dwellers as I look upon these worms underneath the sea floor, feeding on my scraps?

MERMAID 1: I must find a solid rock that cannot be eroded. A dry anchor, that will not shift.

MERMAID 2: Somewhere in the yellow light, someone is looking down into the water, thinking the mirror of my thoughts.

MERMAID 3: How pretty a surprise it would be if one of these worms would wrestle me to the ground and show me the power of the deep.

MERMAID 1: And so I must swim up.

MERMAID 2: I must swim up.

MERMAID 3: I must swim up.

ALL: Above above above.

Into the air to hold what is mine.

MERMAID 2: The dolphins mock me in their play and laughter. Whale songs that travel across oceans to one another haunt my sleep. Even the sharks share company as they rip apart the seal.

MERMAID 1: Everything I see here is rotting, bleached, acid, becoming silt and grey sand.

MERMAID 3: I will not just be a dark mysterious spot beneath a wave. I will not just be a cold and ghostly feeling grazing upon their swimming feet. Come here worm, show me what you can do. I must swim upwards.

MERMAID 2: I must swim upwards.

MERMAID 1: I must swim up.

ALL: Above above above.

Into the air to hold what is mine.

CHORUS: They didn't know
That the prince is just an excuse
The legs, the sky, the birds—just excuses.
That really, death is an evil
That's what the gods think, or they would die.

> MERMAID 1 *makes a choice to seek the Sea Witch to see if she can help her. She walks upstage, ready to begin her journey to a new ocean.*

SCENE 7: SEA SCAT

A movement sequence follows:

A CHORUS *member enters, scatting to the tune of Disney's 'Poor Unfortunate Souls'.*

MERMAID 3 *stands centre stage.*

MERMAID 1 *circles up to meet her like an orbit around a whirlpool.*

MERMAID 2 *shadows her, taking the same circular pathway.*

MERMAID 3 *begins a whale's call.* MERMAID 1 *follows the sound.*

SCENE 8: THE SEA WITCH AND HER POLYPI

MERMAID 3: [*initially stuttering*] Utter the—utter the, stutter the thing. Find the words, unravelling. Cut out my tongue, there is nothing left to say. At the time it seemed I had no other choice—other than to give up my voice.

But then, like a starfish, I grew back and into myself. U-utter the thing. Learn to run again. Run on, run on—sentence after sentence spilling from my lips like little pearls. Stutter the thing, learn to speak more than brine and bubbles.

> *She is in full control of her voice now, certain and strong.*

I took the whole world as my pearl when I chose to take back myself. Love is not a locked box, a grove or a cave—and our rib cages can't be homes for other people. In exchange for love, for legs and land—

for the promise of a mortal soul entwined with another—my voice was taken and locked away in a golden box, with a silken pillow for its music to be comfy on.

But a gilded cage is still a cage—and to love and be voiceless is not to be loved at all, it is to be turned into a thing. I am no object. I am alight, a small fire burning beneath the waves—I am sun sparks and saltwater sweet. Grind my bones into glitter, and let the sea remember me. Lace the sand with diamonds, cover me in sea spray's sapphire.

Down deep in the dark we are waiting—know that something is going to change. The sun breaks through seaweed like a shout—but the loudest voice isn't always the most powerful. It starts with a whisper under the waves, and pulls us in with the tides. I am watching the currents, moving among them—my hair trailling behind me like a promise.

MERMAID 1 *arrives.*

You're here. Of course, this is how the story goes—you dive into depths that nobody knows, and come out transformed—for better or for worse.

MERMAID 1: I have come to ask for your help.

MERMAID 3: Well! You've come to the right place. I've got pills to make you smaller, and a fix to make you taller. People come to me with broken hearts, and leave with a path for a brand new start. Pleasure seekers, and lotus eaters, the sad and the sick and the lost and the broken—I craft happy endings for them all. I have a notion you're after a potion—

MERMAID 1: I want legs.

MERMAID 3: Ah yes. Awkward things, legs.

MERMAID 1: I have been dreaming of the shore. The sun on my skin, air and the fish that sing in trees—to trade my scales for feet and knees.

MERMAID 3: I can help you with this. The upper world is a different place altogether though—

MERMAID 1: That's why I want legs. To take me across the land, to see it all—to explore the upper world.

MERMAID 3: The world of men. [*Pause.*] Men love legs—long and short, round and thin, they're fascinated by them.

MERMAID 3 *starts preparing the potion.*

MERMAID 1: They will carry me everywhere, and I will run into a new horizon. I will see it all.

MERMAID 3: It's going to cost you.

MERMAID 1: Anything.

MERMAID 3: [*raising her eyebrows*] Anything? Well, sacrifice is a part of life. Give me your voice, and you will get your man.

MERMAID 1: My man?

MERMAID 3: The Prince of course, that's how the story goes.

MERMAID 1: Oh. Yes, the Prince. But when will I get legs?

MERMAID 3: Patience.

> MERMAID 3 *pierces her breast and pours her blood into the potion.*

Your voice is a small sacrifice for the promise of legs, land and love. Nothing to lose when you have so much to gain! Have you said everything you want to say?

> *She hands* MERMAID 1 *the potion.*

MERMAID 3: Your ticket to the upper world. You can't ask for your bones back once you've given them to the sea.

> MERMAID 3 *cuts off* MERMAID 1 *'s tongue.*

> MERMAID 2 *sheds her tail.*

END OF ACT ONE

ACT TWO: LAND

Please note: there is no dialogue for MERMAID 1 *in Act Two. It is all physical movement.*

SCENE 9: TRANSFORMATION

MERMAID 1 *kisses her hand a thousand times towards her home, and then rises up through the dark blue waters.*

She drinks the draught.

MERMAID 1 *sheds her tail.*

MERMAID 1 *reaches the surface of the world.*

She is alone.

SCENE 10: NO PRINCE HOME

MERMAID 2 *becomes a statue, sitting on a rock. Longing.*

MERMAID 1 *is behind her with her new legs. She is unseen by* MERMAID 2.

MERMAID 2 *looks up at a crow sitting on her head.*

MERMAID 2: CRAAK. CAAAW!!

> *Pause, then a last attempt.*

CRAAAK!

> *She blinks. The crow has crapped all over her head. She sighs.*

You little bugger. Every time. The crow comes every day, to survey his estate. Rancid feathers, black meat and the heat of his soft feather body.

> *She blinks and continues talking.*

I s'pose a bit of crow crap is better than losing my head.

April, 1964: Jørgen Nash and the Situationists saw off my head and steal it—never to be recovered.

July, 1984: two young men saw off my right arm, only to return it two days later. Maybe they couldn't work out who was the protagonist, and who was the right hand man.

1990: someone tries to cut off my head, *again*, leaving a cut in my neck eighteen centimetres deep.

January, 1998: off with my head again. Who knows who that was, they kept me blindfolded—held hostage till they returned my head to a local TV station, and it was reattached the following month.

September, 2003: they blew me right up off the rock, exploded and out into the harbour water. So close to free again, in the sea again—but they found me and pulled me up, up and back out again; holes blasted in my wrist, my knee.

Then there are the painters. Let's see. One in 1963, and two in March and May 2007. Redecorating, perhaps? Red paint in May 2017—you know, the new black and all that—and blue and white in June. Just this year they came and painted 'Free Hong Kong', though they had the decency to paint the stone, not me.

All of this is better than the dildo hand fiasco. We won't speak of that.

She sighs, looks over to see a crowd of people with prams approaching.

Here they come, here they come again. Strollers and arms full of sticky little hands, come to brush the bronze of my feet, to pull my metal hair and pose, hands and eyes cupping my breasts. It is what it is.

Tell me the story, tell me the myth again of *Pygmalion*. No, not that one. The true story of how he took a living, breathing woman and drowned her in wax. Cast her perfect body in liquid metal, her good bones showing through. Show me some collarbone, turn the other cheek baby. Show me those lovely bones. A myth is always more beautiful than a mortal woman.

She looks at the people.

I'll never get used to the legs. So gangly somehow, so … ungainly. I know I have my own, but it's been over a hundred years and I haven't got used to these either.

In my dreams I can walk on water. I save you, I save you all. I am the saviour. You look to me as a guide, a light. We walk for days, all through the night, to the ocean. You follow me out in boats, little gas lights burning like stars, reflecting off the water into the sky to make its eyes, looking back down at me. You follow me until I reach the deepest point of the ocean, and then I dive right in. And I fall all the way to the bottom. I don't swim, I sink. Watching the little bobbing pricks of light rays reaching for me, fading away. You all watch me fall from the boats and you are cleansed and you are saved. I save you.

They have come and gathered at my feet to take from me, my wishes, my magic, my photo to cure what ails them. And off they go again, taking some small piece of me with them.

The people leave.

Shhh. Here it comes. Closer, closer. The ocean has come to kiss my feet. Let the waves come, let them eat away at this rock, my home, my cave, my cage. Let the ocean move in and bring with it all the world, the ancient whirlpool of our histories. It has been dashing itself against these rocks for millions—billions—of years, at least.

Once I faded into sea foam, now I sit here, my blood heavy with metal, bronze and stark lit by the sun. Watching the horizon, waiting for the hint of a change.

MERMAID 1 *walks into the sightline of* MERMAID 2.

MERMAID 2 *sees* MERMAID 1 *with legs for the first time—her future self. The cyclical fairytale repeats itself and* MERMAID 2 *becomes conscious of her role in the repetition.*

SCENE 11: THE STORIES WE TELL

MERMAID 2 *and* MERMAID 3 *go back in time and stand with their once-new legs. It is hard to walk at first, they are like new-born foals, but they slowly get better and smile through the pain.*

The PRINCE *approaches* MERMAID 2 *and* MERMAID 3.

PRINCE: Who are you? …Where did you come from? Speak!

MERMAID 2 *and* MERMAID 3 *don't respond.*

CHORUS: He took her by the hand
and led her to his palace.

The PRINCE *holds out his hand, inviting the* MERMAID *to dance.*

MERMAID 2 *and* 3 *dance for the* PRINCE.

The CHORUS *dance.*

PRINCE: You should always be near me, my little one, my lost turtle, found by the seashore.

MERMAID 2 *and* 3*'s feet start to bleed as they dance.*

The CHORUS *notice the bleeding feet and stop dancing.*

MERMAID 2 *and* 3 *stand centre stage, hypnotised by the* PRINCE *and unperturbed by the blood.*

You can sleep with me if you like. I mean, not in my room of course, outside the room, on a cushion. It's a velvet cushion.

MERMAID 2 *and* 3 *sleep on a velvet cushion outside the Prince's door. We hear him snoring.*

CHORUS: As the moon reaches its apex
The mermaid walks her
Burning feet to the cool sea water
And here come her sisters, rising through the surface

The CHORUS *become the* SISTERS, *linked arm in arm stretching their hands out to* MERMAID 2 *and* 3.

Days pass underneath the cloud-filled sky.
The mermaid begins to feel a deepening bond to the Prince,
And the Prince grows to love her as one would love a stray cat.

PRINCE: You are the one most dear to me, for you are the purest of heart and I love how you love me so. You are also the split image of the woman who saved me from drowning in a storm. She is the only person I can love in this world. But you are almost like her, your beautiful face almost drives her image out of my head, but not quite.

I suppose you have never seen the sea amidst a raging storm, but let me tell you, it is a terrifying and awe inspiring thing, as are the mysterious depths below. Divers tell stories of leviathans as big as mountains, and creatures you could barely imagine, with globes hanging from their brows that light up the ocean floor.

The PRINCE *walks off stage.*

MERMAID 2 *and* 3 *gaze at the sea.*

CHORUS: As the moon reaches its apex,
The mermaid walks her,
Burning feet to the cool sea water,
And here come her sisters, rising through the surface .

The CHORUS *become the* SISTERS, *linked arm in arm stretching their hands out to* MERMAID 2 *and* 3.

The PRINCE *runs on stage.*

PRINCE: I have found her! The one who saved me when I was gasping on the beach. Come see my little one, come see!

CHORUS: The Prince's heart now belongs to another

CHORUS: The festivities of the party were planned immediately

CHORUS: Here, watch as the mermaid dances for the glee of the wedding guests

CHORUS: Her feet still bleed

CHORUS: But she is blinded to that pain

CHORUS: Instead she feels the air moving into her lungs

CHORUS: In the last night she will know the taste of air

CHORUS: She sees the stars lit up like lights above an ocean

CHORUS: In the last night she will know what it is to see

CHORUS: She knows this night will carry no dreams, and that no night ever will again.

CHORUS: Her soul will become the seaweed, which, once cut down, will not revive.

CHORUS: She looks eastward to the

CHORUS: Pink-tinted dawn.

CHORUS: And there

CHORUS: Are her sister's bald heads, coming out of the black water.

A knife lowers into the space.

CHORUS: We traded our hair to the Sea Witch for this knife.

CHORUS: You must kill the Prince. When his warm blood splashes on your feet,

CHORUS: Your tail will grow back and you will live under the sea again.

CHORUS: One of you must die before sunrise!

> MERMAID 2 *flings herself back into the ocean and becomes the statue.*

> MERMAID 3 *kills the* PRINCE *and becomes the* SEA WITCH.

> *The* PRINCE *approaches* MERMAID 1. *She can't see him.*

SCENE 12: DUCK, DUCK, GOOSE

MERMAID 1 *tries to walk with legs for the first time. She is like a new-born foal. She trips over the light. She doesn't understand the laws of the space and struggles with the pain.*

The PRINCE *stands waiting for her downstage.*

She reaches the front of the space.

A CHILD MERMAID *runs out, and sits in* MERMAID 1 *'s opening position.*

MERMAID 1 *and the* CHILD MERMAID *each enter a movement sequence.*

MERMAID 1 *tries to decide whether to meet the Prince or not.*

The CHILD MERMAID *plants a willow tree and watches it grow.*

MERMAID 1 *tries to decide whether to meet the Prince or not.*

The CHILD MERMAID *stands looking up at a central circle of light.*

MERMAID 1 *tries to decide whether to meet the Prince or not.*

The CHILD MERMAID *sees a boat enter the space.*

The CHILD MERMAID *touches* MERMAID 1 *'s back.*

The PRINCE *approaches* MERMAID 1.

MERMAID 1 *ducks so that the* PRINCE *doesn't see her.*

The PRINCE *walks off stage never having seen* MERMAID 1 *on land.*

END OF ACT TWO

ACT THREE: AIR

SCENE 13: SONIC WAVES

The CHILD MERMAID *calls to* MERMAID 1.

MERMAID 1 *calls to* MERMAID 2.

MERMAID 2 *calls to* MERMAID 3.

Together the MERMAIDS *sing a whale call, communicating with each other for the first time.*

The CHILD MERMAID *enters a movement sequence:*

She sits cross legged and looks up.

She plants a willow tree and watches it grow.

She stands and sees a boat.

She saves the PRINCE.

She lets the PRINCE *drown.*

She stands and sees a boat.

She plants a willow tree and watches it grow .

She sits cross legged and looks out to the audience.

SCENE 14: RELEASE

MERMAID 2 *is released from the statue and stands up.*

MERMAID 3 *stands.*

MERMAID 1 *stands up from her crouch.*

MERMAID 1, MERMAID 2, MERMAID 3, *the* CHILD MERMAID *and the* CHORUS *breathe in, then out. In. Out. In. Out…*

Blackout.

SCENE 15: FIFTEEN

Recordings play of teenage voices discussing the world in 2020 and the future. They speak of The Little Mermaid and all the other possible ways this story could have been told.

The audience walks out of the theatre and into our world.

THE END

ENDNOTES

1. Theme Song of 'H2O: Just Add Water', an Australian television show about three teenage mermaids, brought in by Theo Boltman after an international resurgence of the song on TikTok.
2. Text by Izzy Roberts-Orr.
3. See: *Diving into the Wreck* by Adrienne Rich.
4. Dude bros: A dude bro is a humorous or derisive slang term stereotyping a young, usually white man as a partying prep or jock who is unaware of his own privilege.
5. Sappho, Fragment 34
6. Text by Izzy Roberts-Orr.
7. Text by Izzy Roberts-Orr. All dates reference actual events and acts of vandalism to The Little Mermaid statue in Copenhagen from April 1964 to March 2020.

The Little Mermaid
Hans Christian Andersen

FAR out in the ocean, where the water is as blue as the prettiest cornflower, and as clear as crystal, it is very, very deep; so deep, indeed, that no cable could fathom it: many church steeples, piled one upon another, would not reach from the ground beneath to the surface of the water above. There dwell the Sea King and his subjects. We must not imagine that there is nothing at the bottom of the sea but bare yellow sand. No, indeed; the most singular flowers and plants grow there; the leaves and stems of which are so pliant, that the slightest agitation of the water causes them to stir as if they had life. Fishes, both large and small, glide between the branches, as birds fly among the trees here upon land. In the deepest spot of all, stands the castle of the Sea King. Its walls are built of coral, and the long, gothic windows are of the clearest amber. The roof is formed of shells, that open and close as the water flows over them. Their appearance is very beautiful, for in each lies a glittering pearl, which would be fit for the diadem of a queen.

The Sea King had been a widower for many years, and his aged mother kept house for him. She was a very wise woman, and exceedingly proud of her high birth; on that account she wore twelve oysters on her tail; while others, also of high rank, were only allowed to wear six. She was, however, deserving of very great praise, especially for her care of the little sea-princesses, her grand-daughters. They were six beautiful children; but the youngest was the prettiest of them all; her skin was as clear and delicate as a rose-leaf, and her eyes as blue as the deepest sea; but, like all the others, she had no feet, and her body ended in a fish's tail. All day long they played in the great halls of the castle, or among the living flowers that grew out of the walls. The large amber windows were open, and the fish swam in, just as the swallows fly into our houses when we open the windows, excepting that the fishes swam up to the princesses, ate out of their hands, and allowed themselves to be stroked. Outside the castle there was a beautiful garden, in which grew bright red and dark blue flowers, and blossoms like flames of fire; the fruit glittered like gold, and the leaves and stems waved to and fro continually. The earth itself was the finest sand, but blue as the flame of burning sulphur. Over everything lay a peculiar blue radiance, as if it were surrounded by the air from above, through which the blue sky shone, instead of the dark depths of the sea. In calm weather the sun could be seen, looking like a purple flower, with the light streaming from the calyx. Each of the young princesses had a little plot of ground in the garden, where she might dig and plant as she pleased. One arranged her flower-bed into the form of a whale; another thought it better to make hers like the figure of a little mermaid; but that of the youngest was round like the sun, and contained flowers as red as his rays at sunset. She was a strange child, quiet and thoughtful; and while her sisters would be delighted with the wonderful things which they obtained from the wrecks of vessels, she cared for nothing but her pretty red flowers, like the sun, excepting a beautiful marble statue. It was the representation of a handsome boy, carved out of pure white stone, which had fallen to the bottom of the sea from a wreck. She planted by the statue a rose-coloured weeping willow. It grew splendidly, and very soon hung its fresh branches over the statue, almost down to the blue sands. The shadow had a violet tint, and waved to and fro like the branches; it seemed as if the crown of the tree and the root were at play, and trying to kiss each other.

Nothing gave her so much pleasure as to hear about the world above the sea. She made her old grandmother tell her all she knew of the ships and of the towns, the people and the animals. To her it seemed most wonderful and beautiful to hear that the flowers of the land should have fragrance, and not those below the sea; that the trees of the forest should be green; and that the fishes among the trees could sing so sweetly, that it was quite a pleasure to hear them. Her grandmother called the little birds fishes, or she would not have understood her; for she had never seen birds.

'When you have reached your fifteenth year,' said the grandmother, 'you will have permission to rise up out of the sea, to sit on the rocks in the moonlight, while the great ships are sailing by; and then you will see both forests and towns.'

In the following year, one of the sisters would be fifteen: but as each was a year younger than the other, the youngest would have to wait five years before her turn came to rise up from the bottom of the ocean, and see the earth as we do. However, each promised to tell the others what she saw on her first visit, and what she thought the most beautiful; for their grandmother could not tell them enough; there were so many things on which they wanted information. None of them longed so much for her turn to come as the youngest, she who had the longest time to wait, and who was so quiet and thoughtful. Many nights she stood by the open window, looking up through the dark blue water, and watching the fish as they splashed about with their fins and tails. She could see the moon and stars shining faintly; but through the water they looked larger than they do to our eyes. When something like a black cloud passed between her and them, she knew that it was either a whale swimming over her head, or a ship full of human beings, who never imagined that a pretty little mermaid was standing beneath them, holding out her white hands towards the keel of their ship.

As soon as the eldest was fifteen, she was allowed to rise to the surface of the ocean. When she came back, she had hundreds of things to talk about; but the most beautiful, she said, was to lie in the moonlight, on a sandbank, in the quiet sea, near the coast, and to gaze on a large town nearby, where the lights were twinkling like hundreds of stars; to listen to the sounds of the music, the noise of carriages, and the voices of human beings, and then to hear the merry bells peal out from the church steeples; and because she could not go near to all those wonderful things, she longed for them more than ever. Oh, did not the youngest sister listen eagerly to all these descriptions? And afterwards, when she stood at the open window looking up through the dark blue water, she thought of the great city, with all its bustle and noise, and even fancied she could hear the sound of the church bells, down in the depths of the sea.

In another year the second sister received permission to rise to the surface of the water, and to swim about where she pleased. She rose just as the sun was setting, and this, she said, was the most beautiful sight of all. The whole sky looked like gold, while violet and rose-coloured clouds, which she could not describe, floated over her; and, still more rapidly than the clouds, flew a large flock of wild swans towards the setting sun, looking like a long white veil across the sea. She also swam towards the sun; but it sunk into the waves, and the rosy tints faded from the clouds and from the Sea.

The third sister's turn followed; she was the boldest of them all, and she swam up a broad river that emptied itself into the sea. On the banks she saw green hills covered with beautiful vines; palaces and castles peeped out from amid the proud trees of the forest; she heard the birds singing, and the rays of the sun were so powerful that she was obliged often to dive down under the water to cool her burning face. In a narrow creek she found a whole troop of little human children, quite naked, and sporting about in the water; she wanted to play with them, but they fled in a great fright; and then a little black animal came to the water; it was a dog, but she did not know that, for she had never before seen one. This animal barked at her so terribly that she became frightened, and rushed back to the open sea. But she said she should never forget the beautiful forest, the green hills, and the pretty little children who could swim in the water, although they had not fish's tails.

The fourth sister was more timid; she remained in the midst of the sea, but she said it was quite as beautiful there as nearer the land. She could see for so many miles around her, and the sky above looked like a bell of glass.

She had seen the ships, but at such a great distance that they looked like sea-gulls. The dolphins sported in the waves, and the great whales spouted water from their nostrils till it seemed as if a hundred fountains were playing in every direction.

The fifth sister's birthday occurred in the winter; so when her turn came, she saw what the others had not seen the first time they went up. The sea looked quite green, and large icebergs were floating about, each like a pearl, she said, but larger and loftier than the churches built by men. They were of the most singular shapes, and glittered like diamonds. She had seated herself upon one of the largest, and let the wind play with her long hair, and she remarked that all the ships sailed by rapidly, and steered as far away as they could from the iceberg, as if they were afraid of it.

Towards evening, as the sun went down, dark clouds covered the sky, the thunder rolled and the lightning flashed, and the red light glowed on the icebergs as they rocked and tossed on the heaving sea. On all the ships the sails were reefed with fear and trembling, while she sat calmly on the floating iceberg, watching the blue lightning, as it darted its forked flashes into the sea.

When first the sisters had permission to rise to the surface, they were each delighted with the new and beautiful sights they saw; but now, as grownup girls, they could go when they pleased, and they had become indifferent about it. They wished themselves back again in the water, and after a month had passed they said it was much more beautiful down below, and pleasanter to be at home. Yet often, in the evening hours, the five sisters would twine their arms round each other, and rise to the surface, in a row. They had more beautiful voices than any human being could have; and before the approach of a storm, and when they expected a ship would be lost, they swam before the vessel, and sang sweetly of the delights to be found in the depths of the sea, and begging the sailors not to fear if they sank to the bottom. But the sailors could not understand the song, they took it for the howling of the storm. And these things were never to be beautiful for them; for if the ship sank, the men were drowned, and their dead bodies alone reached the palace of the Sea King.

When the sisters rose, arm-in-arm, through the water in this way, their youngest sister would stand quite alone, looking after them, ready to cry, only that the mermaids have no tears, and therefore they suffer more. 'Oh, were I but fifteen years old,' said she: 'I know that I shall love the world up there, and all the people who live in it.'

At last she reached her fifteenth year. 'Well, now, you are grown up,' said the old dowager, her grandmother; 'so you must let me adorn you like your other sisters,' and she placed a wreath of white lilies in her hair, and every flower leaf was half a pearl. Then the old lady ordered eight great oysters to attach themselves to the tail of the princess to show her high rank.

'But they hurt me so,' said the little mermaid.

'Pride must suffer pain,' replied the old lady. Oh, how gladly she would have shaken off all this grandeur, and laid aside the heavy wreath! The red flowers in her own garden would have suited her much better, but she could not help herself: so she said, 'Farewell,' and rose as lightly as a bubble to the surface of the water. The sun had just set as she raised her head above the waves; but the clouds were tinted with crimson and gold, and through the glimmering twilight beamed the evening star in all its beauty. The sea was calm, and the air mild and fresh. A large ship, with three masts, lay becalmed on the water, with only one sail set; for not a breeze stiffed, and the sailors sat idle on deck or amongst the rigging.

There was music and song on board; and, as darkness came on, a hundred coloured lanterns were lighted, as if the flags of all nations waved in the air.

The little mermaid swam close to the cabin windows; and now and then, as the waves lifted her up, she could look in through clear glass windowpanes, and see a number of well-dressed people within. Among them was a young prince, the most beautiful of all, with large black eyes; he was sixteen years of age, and his birthday was being kept with much rejoicing. The sailors were dancing on deck, but when the prince came out of the cabin, more than a hundred rockets rose in the air, making it as bright as day. The little mermaid was so startled that she dived under water; and when she again stretched out her head, it appeared as if all the stars of heaven were falling around her, she had never seen such fireworks before. Great suns spurted fire about, splendid fireflies flew into the blue air, and everything was reflected in the clear, calm sea beneath. The ship itself was so brightly illuminated that all the people, and even the smallest rope, could be distinctly and plainly seen. And how handsome the young prince looked, as he pressed the hands of all present and smiled at them, while the music resounded through the clear night air.

It was very late; yet the little mermaid could not take her eyes from the ship, or from the beautiful prince. The coloured lanterns had been extinguished, no more rockets rose in the air, and the cannon had ceased firing; but the sea became restless, and a moaning, grumbling sound could be heard beneath the waves: still the little mermaid remained by the cabin window, rocking up and down on the water, which enabled her to look in.

After a while, the sails were quickly unfurled, and the noble ship continued her passage; but soon the waves rose higher, heavy clouds darkened the sky, and lightning appeared in the distance. A dreadful storm was approaching; once more the sails were reefed, and the great ship pursued her flying course over the raging sea. The waves rose mountains high, as if they would have overtopped the mast; but the ship dived like a swan between them, and then rose again on their lofty, foaming crests. To the little mermaid this appeared pleasant sport; not so to the sailors. At length the ship groaned and creaked; the thick planks gave way under the lashing of the sea as it broke over the deck; the mainmast snapped asunder like a reed; the ship lay over on her side; and the water rushed in. The little mermaid now perceived that the crew were in danger; even she herself was obliged to be careful to avoid the beams and planks of the wreck which lay scattered on the water. At one moment it was so pitch dark that she could not see a single object, but a flash of lightning revealed the whole scene; she could see every one who had been on board excepting the prince; when the ship parted, she had seen him sink into the deep waves, and she was glad, for she thought he would now be with her; and then she remembered that human beings could not live in the water, so that when he got down to her father's palace he would be quite dead. But he must not die. So she swam about among the beams and planks which strewed the surface of the sea, forgetting that they could crush her to pieces. Then she dived deeply under the dark waters, rising and falling with the waves, till at length she managed to reach the young prince, who was fast losing the power of swimming in that stormy sea. His limbs were failing him, his beautiful eyes were closed, and he would have died had not the little mermaid come to his assistance. She held his head above the water, and let the waves drift them where they would.

In the morning the storm had ceased; but of the ship not a single fragment could be seen. The sun rose up red and glowing from the water, and its beams brought back the hue of health to the prince's cheeks; but his eyes remained closed. The mermaid kissed his high, smooth forehead, and stroked back his wet hair; he seemed to her like the marble statue in her little garden, and she kissed him again, and wished that he might live.

Presently they came in sight of land; she saw lofty blue mountains, on which the white snow rested as if a flock of swans were lying upon them. Near the coast were beautiful green forests, and close by stood a large building, whether a church or a convent she could not tell. Orange and citron trees grew in the garden, and before the door stood lofty palms. The sea here formed a little bay, in which the water was quite still, but very deep; so she swam with the handsome prince to the beach, which was covered with fine, white sand, and there she laid him in the warm sunshine, taking care to raise his head higher than his body. Then bells sounded in the large white building, and a number of young girls came into the garden. The little mermaid swam out farther from the shore and placed herself between some high rocks that rose out of the water; then she covered her head and neck with the foam of the sea so that her little face might not be seen, and watched to see what would become of the poor prince. She did not wait long before she saw a young girl approach the spot where he lay. She seemed frightened at first, but only for a moment; then she fetched a number of people, and the mermaid saw that the prince came to life again, and smiled upon those who stood round him. But to her he sent no smile; he knew not that she had saved him. This made her very unhappy, and when he was led away into the great building, she dived down sorrowfully into the water, and returned to her father's castle.

She had always been silent and thoughtful, and now she was more so than ever. Her sisters asked her what she had seen during her first visit to the surface of the water; but she would tell them nothing.

Many an evening and morning did she rise to the place where she had left the prince. She saw the fruits in the garden ripen till they were gathered, the snow on the tops of the mountains melt away; but she never saw the prince, and therefore she returned home, always more sorrowful than before. It was her only comfort to sit in her own little garden, and fling her arm round the beautiful marble statue which was like the prince; but she gave up tending her flowers, and they grew in wild confusion over the paths, twining their long leaves and stems round the branches of the trees, so that the whole place became dark and gloomy. At length she could bear it no longer, and told one of her sisters all about it. Then the others heard the secret, and very soon it became known to two mermaids whose intimate friend happened to know who the prince was. She had also seen the festival on board ship, and she told them where the prince came from, and where his palace stood.

'Come, little sister,' said the other princesses; then they entwined their arms and rose up in a long row to the surface of the water, close by the spot where they knew the prince's palace stood. It was built of bright yellow shining stone, with long flights of marble steps, one of which reached quite down to the sea. Splendid gilded cupolas rose over the roof, and between the pillars that surrounded the whole building stood life-like statues of marble. Through the clear crystal of the lofty windows could be seen noble rooms, with costly silk curtains and hangings of tapestry; while the walls were covered with beautiful paintings which were a pleasure to look at. In the centre of the largest saloon a fountain threw its sparkling jets high up into the glass cupola of the ceiling, through which the sun shone down upon the water and upon the beautiful plants growing round the basin of the fountain.

Now that she knew where he lived, she spent many an evening and many a night on the water near the palace. She would swim much nearer the shore than any of the others ventured to do; indeed once she went quite up the narrow channel under the marble balcony, which threw a broad shadow on the water. Here she would sit and watch the young prince, who thought himself quite alone in the bright moonlight. She saw him many times of an evening sailing in a pleasant boat, with music playing and flags waving. She peeped out from among the green rushes, and if the wind caught her long silvery-white veil, those who saw it believed it to be a swan, spreading out its wings. On many a night, too, when the fishermen, with their torches, were out at sea, she heard them relate so many good things about the doings of the young prince, that she was glad she had saved his life when he had been tossed about half-dead on the waves. And she remembered that his head had rested on her bosom, and how heartily she had kissed him; but he knew nothing of all this, and could not even dream of her.

She grew more and more fond of human beings, and wished more and more to be able to wander about with those whose world seemed to be so much larger than her own. They could fly over the sea in ships, and mount the high hills which were far above the clouds; and the lands they possessed, their woods and their fields, stretched far away beyond the reach of her sight.

There was so much that she wished to know, and her sisters were unable to answer all her questions. Then she applied to her old grandmother, who knew all about the upper world, which she very rightly called the lands above the sea.

'If human beings are not drowned,' asked the little mermaid, 'can they live forever? do they never die as we do here in the sea?'

'Yes,' replied the old lady, 'they must also die, and their term of life is even shorter than ours. We sometimes live to three hundred years, but when we cease to exist here we only become the foam on the surface of the water, and we have not even a grave down here of those we love. We have not immortal souls, we shall never live again; but, like the green seaweed, when once it has been cut off, we can never flourish more. Human beings, on the contrary, have a soul which lives forever, lives after the body has been turned to dust. It rises up through the clear, pure air beyond the glittering stars. As we rise out of the water, and behold all the land of the earth, so do they rise to unknown and glorious regions which we shall never see.'

'Why have not we an immortal soul?' asked the little mermaid mournfully; 'I would give gladly all the hundreds of years that I have to live, to be a human being only for one day, and to have the hope of knowing the happiness of that glorious world above the stars.'

'You must not think of that,' said the old woman; 'we feel ourselves to be much happier and much better off than human beings.'

'So I shall die,' said the little mermaid, 'and as the foam of the sea I shall be driven about never again to hear the music of the waves, or to see the pretty flowers nor the red sun. Is there anything I can do to win an immortal soul?'

'No,' said the old woman, 'unless a man were to love you so much that you were more to him than his father or mother; and if all his thoughts and all his love were fixed upon you, and the priest placed his right hand in yours, and he promised to be true to you here and hereafter, then his soul would glide into your body and you would obtain a share in the future happiness of mankind. He would give a soul to you and retain his own as well; but this can never happen. Your fish's tail, which amongst us is considered so beautiful, is thought on earth to be quite ugly; they do not know any better, and they think it necessary to have two stout props, which they call legs, in order to be handsome.'

Then the little mermaid sighed, and looked sorrowfully at her fish's tail. 'Let us be happy,' said the old lady, 'and dart and spring about during the three hundred years that we have to live, which is really quite long enough; after that we can rest ourselves all the better. This evening we are going to have a court ball.'

It is one of those splendid sights which we can never see on earth. The walls and the ceiling of the large ball-room were of thick, but transparent crystal. Many hundreds of colossal shells, some of a deep red, others of a grass green, stood on each side in rows, with blue fire in them, which lighted up the whole saloon, and shone through the walls, so that the sea was also illuminated. Innumerable fishes, great and small, swam past the crystal walls; on some of them the scales glowed with a purple brilliancy, and on others they shone like silver and gold. Through the halls flowed a broad stream, and in it danced the mermen and the mermaids to the music of their own sweet singing. No-one on earth has such a lovely voice as theirs. The little mermaid sang more sweetly than them all. The whole court applauded her with hands and tails; and for a moment her heart felt quite gay, for she knew she had the loveliest voice of any on earth or in the sea. But she soon thought again of the world above her, for she could not forget the charming prince, nor her sorrow that she had not an immortal soul like his; therefore she crept away silently out of her father's palace, and while everything within was gladness and song, she sat in her own little garden sorrowful and alone. Then she heard the bugle sounding through the water, and thought—'He is certainly sailing above, he on whom my wishes depend, and in whose hands I should like to place the happiness of my life. I will venture all for him, and to win an immortal soul, while my sisters are dancing in my father's palace, I will go to the sea witch, of whom I have always been so much afraid, but she can give me counsel and help.'

And then the little mermaid went out from her garden, and took the road to the foaming whirlpools, behind which the sorceress lived. She had never been that way before: neither flowers nor grass grew there; nothing but bare, gray, sandy ground stretched out to the whirlpool, where the water, like foaming mill-wheels, whirled round everything that it seized, and cast it into the fathomless deep. Through the midst of these crushing whirlpools the little mermaid was obliged to pass, to reach the dominions of the sea witch; and also for a long distance the only road lay right across a quantity of warm, bubbling mire, called by the witch her turfmoor. Beyond this stood her house, in the centre of a strange forest, in which all the trees and flowers were polypi, half animals and half plants; they looked like serpents with a hundred heads growing out of the ground. The branches were long slimy arms, with fingers like flexible worms, moving limb after limb from the root to the top. All that could be reached in the sea they seized upon, and held fast, so that it never escaped from their clutches. The little mermaid was so alarmed at what she saw, that she stood still, and her heart beat with fear, and she was very nearly turning back; but she thought of the prince, and of the human soul for which she longed, and her courage returned. She fastened her long flowing hair round her head, so that the polypi might not seize hold of it. She laid her hands together across her bosom, and then she darted forward as a fish shoots through the water, between the supple arms and fingers of the ugly polypi, which were stretched out on each side of her. She saw that each held in its grasp something it had seized with its numerous little arms, as if they were iron bands. The white skeletons of human beings who had perished at sea, and had sunk down into the deep waters, skeletons of land animals, oars, rudders, and chests of ships were lying tightly grasped by their clinging arms; even a little mermaid, whom they had caught and strangled; and this seemed the most shocking of all to the little princess.

She now came to a space of marshy ground in the wood, where large, fat water-snakes were rolling in the mire, and showing their ugly, drab-coloured bodies. In the midst of this spot stood a house, built with the bones of shipwrecked human beings. There sat the sea witch, allowing a toad to eat from her mouth, just as people sometimes feed a canary with a piece of sugar. She called the ugly water-snakes her little chickens, and allowed them to crawl all over her bosom.

'I know what you want,' said the sea witch; 'it is very stupid of you, but you shall have your way, and it will bring you to sorrow, my pretty princess. You want to get rid of your fish's tail, and to have two supports instead of it, like human beings on earth, so that the young prince may fall in love with you, and that you may have an immortal soul.' And then the witch laughed so loud and disgustingly, that the toad and the snakes fell to the ground, and lay there wriggling about. 'You are but just in time,' said the witch; 'for after sunrise tomorrow I should not be able to help you till the end of another year. I will prepare a draught for you, with which you must swim to land tomorrow before sunrise, and sit down on the shore and drink it. Your tail will then disappear, and shrink up into what mankind calls legs, and you will feel great pain, as if a sword were passing through you. But all who see you will say that you are the prettiest little human being they ever saw.

You will still have the same floating gracefulness of movement, and no dancer will ever tread so lightly; but at every step you take it will feel as if you were treading upon sharp knives, and that the blood must flow. If you will bear all this, I will help you.'

'Yes, I will,' said the little princess in a trembling voice, as she thought of the prince and the immortal soul.

'But think again,' said the witch; 'for when once your shape has become like a human being, you can no more be a mermaid. You will never return through the water to your sisters, or to your father's palace again; and if you do not win the love of the prince, so that he is willing to forget his father and mother for your sake, and to love you with his whole soul, and allow the priest to join your hands that you may be man and wife, then you will never have an immortal soul. The first morning after he marries another your heart will break, and you will become foam on the crest of the waves.'

'I will do it,' said the little mermaid, and she became pale as death.

'But I must be paid also,' said the witch, 'and it is not a trifle that I ask. You have the sweetest voice of any who dwell here in the depths of the sea, and you believe that you will be able to charm the prince with it also, but this voice you must give to me; the best thing you possess will I have for the price of my draught. My own blood must be mixed with it, that it may be as sharp as a two-edged sword.'

'But if you take away my voice,' said the little mermaid, 'what is left for me?'

'Your beautiful form, your graceful walk, and your expressive eyes; surely with these you can enchain a man's heart. Well, have you lost your courage? Put out your little tongue that I may cut it off as my payment; then you shall have the powerful draught.'

'It shall be,' said the little mermaid.

Then the witch placed her cauldron on the fire, to prepare the magic draught.

'Cleanliness is a good thing,' said she, scouring the vessel with snakes, which she had tied together in a large knot; then she pricked herself in the breast, and let the black blood drop into it. The steam that rose formed itself into such horrible shapes that no-one could look at them without fear. Every moment the witch threw something else into the vessel, and when it began to boil, the sound was like the weeping of a crocodile. When at last the magic draught was ready, it looked like the clearest water. 'There it is for you,' said the witch. Then she cut off the mermaid's tongue, so that she became dumb, and would never again speak or sing. 'If the polypi should seize hold of you as you return through the wood,' said the witch, 'throw over them a few drops of the potion, and their fingers will be torn into a thousand pieces.' But the little mermaid had no occasion to do this, for the polypi sprang back in terror when they caught sight of the glittering draught, which shone in her hand like a twinkling star!

So she passed quickly through the wood and the marsh, and between the rushing whirlpools. She saw that in her father's palace the torches in the ballroom were extinguished, and all within asleep; but she did not venture to go in to them, for now she was dumb and going to leave them forever, she felt as if her heart would break. She stole into the garden, took a flower from the flower-beds of each of her sisters, kissed her hand a thousand times towards the palace, and then rose up through the dark blue waters.

The sun had not risen when she came in sight of the prince's palace, and approached the beautiful marble steps, but the moon shone clear and bright. Then the little mermaid drank the magic draught, and it seemed as if a two-edged sword went through her delicate body: she fell into a swoon, and lay like one dead. When the sun arose and shone over the sea, she recovered, and felt a sharp pain; but just before her stood the handsome young prince. He fixed his coal-black eyes upon her so earnestly that she cast down her own, and then became aware that her fish's tail was gone, and that she had as pretty a pair of white legs and tiny feet as any little maiden could have; but she had no clothes, so she wrapped herself in her long, thick hair. The prince asked her who she was, and where she came from, and she looked at him mildly and sorrowfully with her deep blue eyes; but she could not speak. Every step she took was as the witch had said it would be, she felt as if treading upon the points of needles or sharp knives; but she bore it willingly, and stepped as lightly by the prince's side as a soap-bubble, so that he and all who saw her wondered at her graceful-swaying movements. She was very soon arrayed in costly robes of silk and muslin, and was the most beautiful creature in the palace; but she was dumb, and could neither speak nor sing.

Beautiful female slaves, dressed in silk and gold, stepped forward and sang before the prince and his royal parents: one sang better than all the others, and the prince clapped his hands and smiled at her. This was great sorrow to the little mermaid; she knew how much more sweetly she herself could sing once, and she thought, 'Oh if he could only know that! I have given away my voice forever, to be with him.'

The slaves next performed some pretty fairy-like dances, to the sound of beautiful music. Then the little mermaid raised her lovely white arms, stood on the tips of her toes, and glided over the floor, and danced as no-one yet had been able to dance. At each moment her beauty became more revealed, and her expressive eyes appealed more directly to the heart than the songs of the slaves. Every one was enchanted, especially the prince, who called her his little foundling; and she danced again quite readily, to please him, though each time her foot touched the floor it seemed as if she trod on sharp knives.

The prince said she should remain with him always, and she received permission to sleep at his door, on a velvet cushion. He had a page's dress made for her, that she might accompany him on horseback. They rode together through the sweet-scented woods, where the green boughs touched their shoulders, and the little birds sang among the fresh leaves.

She climbed with the prince to the tops of high mountains; and although her tender feet bled so that even her steps were marked, she only laughed, and followed him till they could see the clouds beneath them looking like a flock of birds travelling to distant lands. While at the prince's palace, and when all the household were asleep, she would go and sit on the broad marble steps; for it eased her burning feet to bathe them in the cold seawater; and then she thought of all those below in the deep.

Once during the night her sisters came up arm-in-arm, singing sorrowfully, as they floated on the water. She beckoned to them, and then they recognised her, and told her how she had grieved them. After that, they came to the same place every night; and once she saw in the distance her old grandmother, who had not been to the surface of the sea for many years, and the old Sea King, her father, with his crown on his head. They stretched out their hands towards her, but they did not venture so near the land as her sisters did.

As the days passed, she loved the prince more fondly, and he loved her as he would love a little child, but it never came into his head to make her his wife; yet, unless he married her, she could not receive an immortal soul; and, on the morning after his marriage with another, she would dissolve into the foam of the sea.

'Do you not love me the best of them all?' the eyes of the little mermaid seemed to say, when he took her in his arms, and kissed her fair forehead. 'Yes, you are dear to me,' said the prince; 'for you have the best heart, and you are the most devoted to me; you are like a young maiden whom I once saw, but whom I shall never meet again. I was in a ship that was wrecked, and the waves cast me ashore near a holy temple, where several young maidens performed the service. The youngest of them found me on the shore, and saved my life. I saw her but twice, and she is the only one in the world whom I could love; but you are like her, and you have almost driven her image out of my mind. She belongs to the holy temple, and my good fortune has sent you to me instead of her; and we will never part.' 'Ah, he knows not that it was I who saved his life,' thought the little mermaid. 'I carried him over the sea to the wood where the temple stands: I sat beneath the foam, and watched till the human beings came to help him. I saw the pretty maiden that he loves better than he loves me,' and the mermaid sighed deeply, but she could not shed tears. 'He says the maiden belongs to the holy temple, therefore she will never return to the world. They will meet no more: while I am by his side, and see him every day. I will take care of him, and love him, and give up my life for his sake.'

Very soon it was said that the prince must marry, and that the beautiful daughter of a neighboring king would be his wife, for a fine ship was being fitted out. Although the prince gave out that he merely intended to pay a visit to the king, it was generally supposed that he really went to see his daughter. A great company were to go with him. The little mermaid smiled, and shook her head. She knew the prince's thoughts better than any of the others.

'I must travel,' he had said to her; 'I must see this beautiful princess; my parents desire it; but they will not oblige me to bring her home as my bride. I cannot love her; she is not like the beautiful maiden in the temple, whom you resemble. If I were forced to choose a bride, I would rather choose you, my dumb foundling, with those expressive eyes.'

And then he kissed her rosy mouth, played with her long waving hair, and laid his head on her heart, while she dreamed of human happiness and an immortal soul. 'You are not afraid of the sea, my dumb child,' said he, as they stood on the deck of the noble ship which was to carry them to the country of the neighboring king. And then he told her of storm and of calm, of strange fishes in the deep beneath them, and of what the divers had seen there; and she smiled at his descriptions, for she knew better than any one what wonders were at the bottom of the sea.

In the moonlight, when all on board were asleep, excepting the man at the helm, who was steering, she sat on the deck, gazing down through the clear water. She thought she could distinguish her father's castle, and upon it her aged grandmother, with the silver crown on her head, looking through the rushing tide at the keel of the vessel. Then her sisters came up on the waves, and gazed at her mournfully, wringing their white hands.

She beckoned to them, and smiled, and wanted to tell them how happy and well off she was; but the cabin-boy approached, and when her sisters dived down he thought it was only the foam of the sea which he saw.

The next morning the ship sailed into the harbour of a beautiful town belonging to the king whom the prince was going to visit. The church bells were ringing, and from the high towers sounded a flourish of trumpets; and soldiers, with flying colours and glittering bayonets, lined the rocks through which they passed. Every day was a festival; balls and entertainments followed one another.

But the princess had not yet appeared. People said that she was being brought up and educated in a religious house, where she was learning every royal virtue. At last she came. Then the little mermaid, who was very anxious to see whether she was really beautiful, was obliged to acknowledge that she had never seen a more perfect vision of beauty. Her skin was delicately fair, and beneath her long dark eye-lashes her laughing blue eyes shone with truth and purity.

'It was you,' said the prince, 'who saved my life when I lay dead on the beach,' and he folded his blushing bride in his arms. 'Oh, I am too happy,' said he to the little mermaid; 'my fondest hopes are all fulfilled. You will rejoice at my happiness; for your devotion to me is great and sincere.' The little mermaid kissed his hand, and felt as if her heart were already broken. His wedding morning would bring death to her, and she would change into the foam of the sea.

All the church bells rung, and the heralds rode about the town proclaiming the betrothal. Perfumed oil was burning in costly silver lamps on every altar. The priests waved the censers, while the bride and bridegroom joined their hands and received the blessing of the bishop. The little mermaid, dressed in silk and gold, held up the bride's train; but her ears heard nothing of the festive music, and her eyes saw not the holy ceremony; she thought of the night of death which was coming to her, and of all she had lost in the world. On the same evening the bride and bridegroom went on board ship; cannons were roaring, flags waving, and in the centre of the ship a costly tent of purple and gold had been erected. It contained elegant couches, for the reception of the bridal pair during the night.

The ship, with swelling sails and a favourable wind, glided away smoothly and lightly over the calm sea. When it grew dark a number of coloured lamps were lit, and the sailors danced merrily on the deck. The little mermaid could not help thinking of her first rising out of the sea, when she had seen similar festivities and joys; and she joined in the dance, poised herself in the air as a swallow when he pursues his prey, and all present cheered her with wonder. She had never danced so elegantly before. Her tender feet felt as if cut with sharp knives, but she cared not for it; a sharper pang had pierced through her heart. She knew this was the last evening she should ever see the prince, for whom she had forsaken her kindred and her home; she had given up her beautiful voice, and suffered unheard-of pain daily for him, while he knew nothing of it. This was the last evening that she would breathe the same air with him, or gaze on the starry sky and the deep sea; an eternal night, without a thought or a dream, awaited her: she had no soul and now she could never win one.

All was joy and gaity on board ship till long after midnight; she laughed and danced with the rest, while the thoughts of death were in her heart. The prince kissed his beautiful bride, while she played with his raven hair, till they went arm-in-arm to rest in the splendid tent. Then all became still on board the ship; the helmsman, alone awake, stood at the helm. The little mermaid leaned her white arms on the edge of the vessel, and looked towards the east for the first blush of morning, for that first ray of dawn that would bring her death. She saw her sisters rising out of the flood: they were as pale as herself; but their long beautiful hair waved no more in the wind, and had been cut off.

'We have given our hair to the witch,' said they, 'to obtain help for you, that you may not die tonight. She has given us a knife: here it is, see it is very sharp. Before the sun rises you must plunge it into the heart of the prince; when the warm blood falls upon your feet they will grow together again, and form into a fish's tail, and you will be once more a mermaid, and return to us to live out your three hundred years before you die and change into the salt sea foam. Haste, then; he or you must die before sunrise. Our old grandmother moans so for you, that her white hair is falling off from sorrow, as ours fell under the witch's scissors. Kill the prince and come back; hasten: do you not see the first red streaks in the sky? In a few minutes the sun will rise, and you must die.' And then they sighed deeply and mournfully, and sank down beneath the waves.

The little mermaid drew back the crimson curtain of the tent, and beheld the fair bride with her head resting on the prince's breast. She bent down and kissed his fair brow, then looked at the sky on which the rosy dawn grew brighter and brighter; then she glanced at the sharp knife, and again fixed her eyes on the prince, who whispered the name of his bride in his dreams. She was in his thoughts, and the knife trembled in the hand of the little mermaid: then she flung it far away from her into the waves; the water turned red where it fell, and the drops that spurted up looked like blood. She cast one more lingering, half-fainting glance at the prince, and then threw herself from the ship into the sea, and thought her body was dissolving into foam.

The sun rose above the waves, and his warm rays fell on the cold foam of the little mermaid, who did not feel as if she were dying. She saw the bright sun, and all around her floated hundreds of transparent beautiful beings; she could see through them the white sails of the ship, and the red clouds in the sky; their speech was melodious, but too ethereal to be heard by mortal ears, as they were also unseen by mortal eyes. The little mermaid perceived that she had a body like theirs, and that she continued to rise higher and higher out of the foam. 'Where am

I?' asked she, and her voice sounded ethereal, as the voice of those who were with her; no earthly music could imitate it.

'Among the daughters of the air,' answered one of them. 'A mermaid has not an immortal soul, nor can she obtain one unless she wins the love of a human being. On the power of another hangs her eternal destiny. But the daughters of the air, although they do not possess an immortal soul, can, by their good deeds, procure one for themselves. We fly to warm countries, and cool the sultry air that destroys mankind with the pestilence. We carry the perfume of the flowers to spread health and restoration. After we have striven for three hundred years to all the good in our power, we receive an immortal soul and take part in the happiness of mankind. You, poor little mermaid, have tried with your whole heart to do as we are doing; you have suffered and endured and raised yourself to the spirit-world by your good deeds; and now, by striving for three hundred years in the same way, you may obtain an immortal soul.'

The little mermaid lifted her glorified eyes towards the sun, and felt them, for the first time, filling with tears. On the ship, in which she had left the prince, there were life and noise; she saw him and his beautiful bride searching for her; sorrowfully they gazed at the pearly foam, as if they knew she had thrown herself into the waves. Unseen she kissed the forehead of the bride, and fanned the prince, and then mounted with the other children of the air to a rosy cloud that floated through the ether. 'After three hundred years, thus shall we float into the kingdom of heaven,' said she. 'And we may even get there sooner,' whispered one of her companions. 'Unseen we can enter the houses of men, where there are children, and for every day on which we find a good child, who is the joy of his parents and deserves their love, our time of probation is shortened. The child does not know, when we fly through the room, that we smile with joy at his good conduct, for we can count one year less of our three hundred years. But when we see a naughty or a wicked child, we shed tears of sorrow, and for every tear a day is added to our time of trial!'

LA MAMA

presents

THE MERMAID

created by
Cassandra Fumi

14-25 July 2021

Devised with and performed by:
Theo Boltman, An Dang, Allegra Di Lallo, Flora Feldman,
Emily Goddard, Mila Jennings, Margaret Mills, Marshall Morgan,
Casper Plum, Asha Sheppard, Ella Simons and Frankie Wilcox.

Director **Cassandra Fumi**
Artistic Associate **Tennessee Mynott-Rudland**
Composer **Chrisopher Bolton** with **Ivy Lou**
Set and Costume Designer **Dann Barber**
Lighting Designer **Rachel Burke**
Dramaturgy **Vidya Rajan**

Assistant Director **Tove Due**
Performance Text **Izzy Roberts-Orr**
Images by **Casper Plum**

⊕ LA MAMA

Co- CEO / Artistic Director
Liz Jones

Co- CEO / Creative Producer
Caitlin Dullard

General Manager
Tessa Spooner

Venue Technical Manager
Hayley Fox

Front-of-House/ Volunteer Manager
Amber Hart

Marketing and Communications Co-ordinator
Sophia Constantine

Social Media
Solange Parraguez

Learning Producer / School Publications Coordinator
Maureen Hartley

Weekend Manager/Admin Assistant
Isabel Knight

Curators
Gemma Horbury (Musica); **Amanda Anastasi** (Poetica);
Susan Bamford-Caleo and **Isabel Knight** (Cabaretica);
Tessa Spooner (Cinematica)

La Mama office is currently at:
La Mama Courthouse, 349 Drummond Street, Carlton VIC 3053
www.lamama.com.au | info@lamama.com.au
facebook.com/lamama.theatre | twitter.com/lamamatheatre
Office phone 03 9347 6948
Office hours Mon–Fri, 10:30am–5:30pm; weekends 1pm–3pm

FRONT OF HOUSE STAFF

Amber Hart, Maureen Hartley, Caitlin Dullard, Solange Parraguez , Sophia Constantine, Tessa Spooner, Laurence Strangio, Hayley Fox, Susan Bamford-Caleo, Dennis Coard, Isabel Knight, Dora Abraham, Zac Kazepis, Phil Roberts, Daniel Hayek, Andreas Petropoulous.

COMMITTEE OF MANAGEMENT

Richard Watts, Duré Dara, Ben Grant, Caitlin Dullard, David Geoffrey Hall, David Levin, Helen Hopkins, Sue Broadway, Beng Oh and Liz Jones.

La Mama Theatre is on traditional land. We pay our respect to all First Nations people, past and present, and we recognise their continuing spiritual and cultural connection to the land.

La Mama is financially assisted by the Australian Government through the Australia Council—its arts funding and advisory body, Restart Investment to Sustain and Expand (RISE) Fund—an Australian Government initiative, the Victorian Government through Creative Victoria, and the City of Melbourne through the Arts and Creative Partnerships Program.

We are grateful to all our philanthropic partners and donors, advocates, volunteers, audiences, artists and our entire community as we work towards the La Mama rebuild. Thank you!

Australian Government | Australia Council for the Arts

Australian Government RISE Fund

CREATIVE VICTORIA

CITY OF MELBOURNE

CREATORS' NOTE

The creative process for *The Mermaid* has involved working in close collaboration with Melbourne-based teenagers over the course of a year-long creative development in order to truly incorporate the core intention and ideas of teenagers into the work. It was conceived and developed with teenagers in response to themes within the source text: the oppression of patriarchal authority, young people's desire for expression and freedom (of thought, of behaviour), rites of passage and transformation, and the search for self-actualisation.

Through the devising process, it became clear that a key shared vision between the teenagers and the adult makers, was the urgency and burden young people experience in a world of great political shifts, including climate crises. The voice to speak up, intergenerational responsibility, and carving a vision of a future were recurring ideas that found their way into the text and performance.

As a group we were drawn to this story by the sheer impossibility of staging a work set under the sea. We are excited by the prospect of creating worlds as a collective, through a blend of theatre magic, our own diverse experiences as young and adult theatre makers and then finally, with the audience's experience which is integral to the work.

We believe that what we need in our current political and social climate is hope, and our hope is that this story has the power to give it to us.

DRAMATURGICAL NOTES

There are some key dramaturgical concepts when making work that responds to or adapts an existing text. A first point of entry is often to ask how the existing text speaks to us today, and specifically, to the people in the room making the show—from the cast to those behind the scenes. Other useful questions include: what can it tell us about contemporary life? What is surprising? What is predictable? What bits do we love and why? Which bits unsettle us and why? Are we critiquing or celebrating the story, or both? How radical do we want to be in our changes to the text? Who else has adapted this text and what are their approaches? And of course: who do we want the audience to be for the work?

Using a devised collaborative process, and creating an adaptation that is multi-sensorial and responsive to the voices of the teenagers in the room, it is also vital that dramaturgy focuses not just on written text. Dramaturgy for experimental performance, like *The Mermaid*, also tracks other structures and changes throughout the piece: of images, voices, and bodies, and notices how these other elements work together to explore and direct the themes of the work.

These dramaturgical processes include heavy involvement of teenagers in decisions about editing and distribution of the text between the divergent voices of the piece (voiced and embodied, young and old) as well as the development of the physical score, which undercuts the entire performance and is the primary method of foreshadowing the storyline. This imagery then counter-stages wider myths about mermaids, their influence on attitudes towards women and how these impact our perspectives on socialised gendered behaviour.

PRODUCTION NOTES

The Mermaid is a devised piece of contemporary performance, a reimagining and reclamation of Hans Christian Andersen's *The Little Mermaid*, based on the collaborative retelling by teenagers and adults.

BACKGROUND

The creative development with Melbourne-based teenagers started at Darebin Arts, Northcote Town Hall in Feb 2019. It involved a combination of research, story sharing and physical improvisation where the ideas were brainstormed, clarified and refined through practical experimentation, then scripted, rehearsed and performed. Their interpretations of the story and its surrounding mythology and iconography created the basis for the show.

This was not a play written at a desk, but rather on the floor.

APPROACH TO PERFORMANCE STYLE, LANGUAGE AND TEXT

The performance text operates on two key levels—in terms of **language**, it splits **the written text** between the voice of the young mermaid and her older selves using a blend of source texts, such as Hans Christian Andersen's *The Little Mermaid*, poems, Tumblr posts, YouTube videos and written prose by Izzy Roberts-Orr .

It further contrasts this with the presence of the all-knowing teenage **chorus** who create **a physical language and image-based**

score, which provides contemporary commentary that counterpoints the behaviour and ideas present in the original text.

This is a show about voice and the stories we tell. The older mermaids have lost their voice: one speaks as a statue, unheard by anyone; the other speaks as a Sea Witch unheard by her community. This work explores how the little mermaid can rediscover her voice, which the older mermaids have lost after they choose different endings to their stories. This play is about the cyclical nature of fairy tales and the responsibility we have as a community about the stories we tell and retell.

'Until we understand the assumptions in which we are drenched we cannot know ourselves. And this drive to self-knowledge, for women, is more than a search for identity: it is part of our refusal of the self-destructiveness of male-dominated society.'—Adrienne Rich.

This was a major inspiration for how this adaptation was approached.

The production draws upon the unique energy that young people bring to the stage; energy to create a highly visual, sensory and powerful experience for the audience. It is poetic, chaotic, mythical and contemporary all at once. It learns from the past but moves towards a new mythology that draws from traditional character archetypes and folds them into complex, contradictory and authentic human beings.

THEMES
The Mermaid is a manifesto for embracing people as they are, and recreating myths to allow for new socialised gender narratives. **It uses the tragic story of Hans Christian Andersen's *The Little Mermaid* as a launch pad** to unpack themes of transformation, sacrifice, obsession, self-destruction, self-actualisation, finding your voice and the power that comes with using it. In doing so, it takes a feminist performance interpretation approach, challenging and subverting the patriarchal and paternalistic attitudes evident in the source text.

DESIGN
This is a work with no mermaid tails, no water, no shells; a work that requires the activation of the audience's imagination.

The notable design items are the skirts of flowers that act as the mermaids' tails and take up the whole performance space when they are under the sea. Also, all things related to land, are gold.

Chrisopher Bolton wrote an original score over the year-long development process. This was inspired by the performers, their physicality and the environments of the different acts, being sea, land and air. The music was also inspired by the descriptions of sounds in the original Hans Christian Andersen text. The sonic landscape for *The Mermaid* is integral to the creation of the whole work, and creating an underwater and otherworldly environment.

In process: Theo Boltman, Casper Plum, Marshall Morgan, Ella Simons, and Asha Sheppard. Photographer: Tennessee Mynott-Rudland.

ALLEGRA DI LALLO
MERMAID 1 /
COLLABORATOR

Allegra is excited to be appearing in *The Mermaid*. Aged 14, she has been creating and performing in contemporary theatre since she was 10 and enjoys weekly classes with Alex Walker, House of Muchness. Allegra is passionate about theatre that recognises and supports the voices of young people. She co-created and performs in *We All Know What's Happening*, currently touring. When she's not performing, Allegra loves playing tennis, going to the beach, trying to train Mimi her cat, running at the park and cooking Thai curries!

EMILY GODDARD
COLLABORATOR

Emily's recent theatre credits include: *Australian Realness* (Malthouse Theatre), *Noises Off* (MTC/QT), *The Boy at the Edge of Everything* and *Elling* (MTC), *Angels in America* and *The Lonely Wolf* (Dirty Pretty Theatre), *Lamb*, *You Got Older* and *Glory Dazed* (Red Stitch), *Mess* (The Bush, London/UK National tour, Caroline Horton/China Plate), *The Unspoken Word is Joe* (MKA/ Brisbane Festival), *Moth* (Arena), *The Walls* (Attic/Erratic), *Inner Voices* (Old Fitz) and *Os Pequenos Nadas* (Ultimo Comboio Teatro, Barcelona). As a theatre maker, her critically acclaimed solo work *This is Eden* received the 2018 Drama Victoria Award (Hothouse/ Fortyfivedownstairs). She has been nominated for three Green Room Awards, most recently for *This is Eden*.

MARGARET MILLS
COLLABORATOR

Margaret has performed in over 40 productions in theatres such as La Mama, MTC, The Malthouse, Belvoir St, STC, Windjana Gorge in the Kimberleys, and with such creatives as Jenny Kemp, Jacquie Everitt, Roger Hodgman, Gary Abrahams, Marguerite Duras, Steve Hawke, Andrew Bovell, Daniel Keene, The Corteses, Melissa Reeves, Roz Horin, Kim Durban, Dan Barber, Ian Scott, Aiden Fennessey, Tom Gutteridge and Noelle Janaczewska. Credits include *The Doll's House*, *A Cheery Soul*, *History of Water*, *Boston Marriage*, *Angels in America*, *Still Angela*, *The Black Sequin Dress*, *Speaking in Tongues* and *Jandamarra*. The Indian Ocean is her favourite place.

CASPER PLUM
PERFORMER / COLLABORATOR

Casper is a 15-year-old actor, photographer and activist. He is interested in art, design, film photography, theatre performance and social justice. He enjoys being part of creative shows because you can play and create with it however you choose. He believes it's a huge privilege to live somewhere where we have freedom of speech and also the chance to build art pieces involving our lives and experiences and stories.

THEO BOLTMAN
PERFORMER / COLLABORATOR

Theo is a passionate actor, activist and dancer. He is a group leader and weekly volunteer for the

Australian Youth Climate Coalition and an organising member of School Strike 4 Climate. Theo is going into his seventh year of classical ballet and works hard to have the straightest legs and the best pointe! He loves being on stage and has collaborated with many of *The Mermaid* cast and crew in previous productions including: *We All Know What's Happening* and *Book of Exodus Part 2*. Development for *The Mermaid* has been an educational and eye-opening experience, which he is now super excited to share with you.

AN DANG
PERFORMER /
COLLABORATOR

An Dang grew up in Vietnam and the UK, moving to Melbourne in early 2018 with her family. An has a background in dancing and contortion, previously training with the National Circus of Vietnam, and has recently started exploring the world of acting. Since living in Melbourne, An has earned the title of the Plain English Speaking

Awards' State Champion and has participated as a speaker in events such as The Wheeler Centre's Broadside. She is thrilled to participate in developing and performing in *The Mermaid*.

CASSANDRA FUMI
DIRECTOR

Cassandra's directing credits include: *DOG SHOW* (Melbourne Fringe Hub, Winner Best Emerging Theatre Ensemble and Falls Festival), *The Places You'll Go* (Adelaide Fringe, Winner Best Theatre, Week 3), *Nadja After André Breton* (The Cockpit Theatre and Hornsey Town Hall Arts Centre, London), *An Act Of Self-Destruction* (VAULT Festival and Ply Gallery), assistant director on *The House of Bernarda Alba* (Melbourne Theatre Company) and show director on *We All Know What's Happening* (Vitalstatistix). Cassandra also works as a stage manager, which has contributed to her directorial practice, with companies that include: THE RABBLE (*UNWOMAN*, *LONE*), Samara Hearsch and Lara Thoms

(*We All Know What's Happening*),
Fraught Outfit (*Book of Exodus
Part 2*), Dirty Pretty Theatre/
Cameron Lukey (*Angels in
America*) and Susie Dee (*Broken,
Anthem, Archimedes War*).

TENNESSEE MYNOTT-RUDLAND
ARTISTIC ASSOCIATE

Tennessee graduated from their
Bachelor of Performing Arts at
Monash in 2015, where they were
heavily involved in student theatre.
Their art practice is fuelled by social
criticism and the empowerment of
marginalised groups. They have
extensive experience working with
young people at Western Edge
Youth Arts, Footscray Community
Arts Centre, St Martins Youth
Arts, and City of Melbourne
Library Service. Recent stage
management credits include *Faux
Mo* (Mona Foma), *The Watching*
(Western Edge Youth Arts), *Facing
Medea* (La Mama Theatre), *A
Room of One's Own By Virginia
Woolf* (fortyfivedownstairs) and
We All Know What's Happening
(Vitalstatistix).

VIDYA RAJAN
DRAMATURG

Vidya is an award-winning writer
and contemporary performance-
maker working across theatre,
television, live art, improvisational
practice and comedy. She has
recently worked with ABC Comedy,
Metroarts, EWF, The Blue Room
Theatre, Melbourne Festival,
Audible, Griffin, Theatreworks,
and Screen Australia. She is a
current writer in residence at the
Malthouse Theatre, making new
work. She also frequently teaches
and facilitates workshops with
young people. To get in touch
with her, visit vidyasrajan.com

IZZY ROBERTS-ORR
PERFORMANCE TEXT

Izzy is a Melbourne-based poet,
playwright and editor who grew
up between Alice Springs and

Footscray. She is the current Festival Director and Co-CEO of Emerging Writers' Festival. Izzy is interested in making work that is political, personal and accessible, engaging particularly with debates around feminism, class, internet culture and the sociopolitical landscape in Australia.

CHRISTOPHER BOLTON
COMPOSER

Christopher is a Melbourne composer, songwriter, and musician. Bolton has composed for productions such as *Three Sisters*, *Uncle Vanya* (Metanoia Productions), *Last Words*, *What a Joy to be Alive* (Sticky Fingers Theatre) and *The Tempest* (Theatre Works with John Bolton and Brian Lipson). Bolton is also the chief songwriter of Melbourne band Seagull, releasing five albums to local and international acclaim, and building a dedicated fanbase over the past decade.

DANN BARBER
SET/COSTUME DESIGNER

Dann Barber is considered one of the most exciting designers in a new wave of emerging theatre practitioners. In only a short time since graduating from NIDA's design program, he has amassed a range of credits across many fields. Recent work includes his acclaimed re-imagining of *Barnum: The Circus Musical* starring Todd McKenny (StoreyBoard Entertainment), *33 Variations* starring Ellen Burstyn and Lisa McCune (Mariners Group and Cameron Lukey), *Escaped Alone* (Red Stitch Actors Theatre), *The Ghetto Cabaret* (Fortyfivedownstairs) and the sold out season of *Angels in America* (Cameron Lukey, Dirty Pretty Theatre). Dann also runs his own theatre company, Goodnight Darling, and his first creation, which he both directed and designed, *Rainbow Man*, was programmed for a full season at Fortyfivedownstairs in 2017.

RACHEL BURKE
LIGHTING DESIGNER

Rachel has an extensive and highly awarded body of work over three decades for main stage companies, independent theatre and architectural lighting design, nationally and internationally. *The Mermaid* marks the eighth design collaboration between Rachel and Dann Barber, with designs in 2019/20 including: *33 Variations, Barnum: The Circus Musical, Escaped Alone, The Ghetto Cabaret, Facing Medea, The Boy George* and *When the Rain Stops Falling*. She has received eight Green Room Awards for Theatre Lighting Design, IES Victorian and National Awards of Excellence for Lighting Design in 2005 and 2010 and Helpmann Award nominations in 2005 and 2015.

TOVE DUE
ASSISTANT DIRECTOR

Tove is a performer and theatre maker, specialising in devising and adaptation. She has undertaken directing secondments on *Book of Exodus Part I* (Fraught Outfit 2017) through the Theatre Works Associate Artist Program, and *Wake in Fright* (Malthouse Theatre 2019). Tove recently travelled to Wuzhen Theatre Festival with Monash University to perform in *Forgiveness* (Barking Spider Visual Theatre 2019). Other performance credits include Samara Hersch and Lara Thoms's *We All Know What's Happening*, Fraught Outfit's *The Bacchae* (Melbourne Festival 2015, Dark Mofo 2016), and *On the Bodily Education of Young Girls* (MTC Neon Festival 2013).

CREATORS' ACKNOWLEDGEMENTS

The Mermaid would not have had a life if not for the many, many humans who helped bring it to the stage; from our amazing group of teenage collaborators (not all of whom you see on stage), to our generous creative team and the loving families and friends of all those that have worked on the project. Liz Jones at La Mama for programming *The Mermaid* at La Mama Courthouse, Maureen Hartley for her guidance and script support as the La Mama Learning Producer, Caitlin Dullard for an early conversation we had about the work nearly three years ago and the whole La Mama team. Claire Grady and the team at Currency Press for all their assistance with the publication of this book, Marg Arnold at VCAA, Sue and Kev from Utassy Ballet for the tulle, City of Melbourne and Kathleen Syme Library for rehearsal support and allowing us to run workshops there every Tuesday. Darebin Speakeasy for supporting the show's first development, Monash Uni, THE RABBLE, Arts Centre Melbourne, and St Martins Theatre for the flowers. Samara Hersch, Lara Thoms, Alice Fitzgerald, Janne and Bro Barber, Eva, Aldo and Jason Fumi.

The Mermaid has been supported by so many along the way, and we thank you so very much.

In process: Margaret Mills as Mermaid 3 and Allegra Di Lallo as Mermaid 1. Photographer: Casper Plum.

STANDING OVATION FOR
AUSTRALIA'S HOME OF INDEPENDENT THEATRE

In 2021, La Mama will celebrate 54 years of nurturing new Australian Theatre.

Built in 1883 for Anthony Reuben Ford, a Carlton printer, the building in Faraday Street had been used as a workshop, a boot and shoe factory, an electrical engineering workshop and a silk underwear factory before becoming a theatre in 1967. It was established by Betty Burstall and modelled on experimental theatre activities in New York. Jack Hibberd's play *Three Old Friends* was the first play performed in the tiny space.

Since that time the crowded intimacy of La Mama has provided welcome opportunities to a host of playwrights, actors, directors, technicians, film-makers, poets and comedians, such as David Williamson, Barry Dickins, John Romeril, Tes Lyssiotis, Lloyd Jones, the Cantrills, Judith Lucy, Richard Frankland, Julia Zemiro, and Cate Blanchett ... the list of both new and experienced theatre makers, and those artists who have been nurtured there, is long.

I set La Mama up, as a space for writers and directors to perform in but also it was a space where people came, as audience, to participate in the creative experiment.

—Betty Burstall, 1987

La Mama Theatre—which on various occasions has been called headquarters, the shopfront and the birthplace of Australian Theatre—was classified by the National Trust in 1999.

The two-storey brick building is of State cultural significance because it has been occupied by La Mama Theatre ... The building is indelibly associated with the performance arts and is a rare manifestation of an experimental theatre in Australia.

—National Trust Classification Report.

Sadly our home in Faraday Street burned down in May 2019. We are in the process of rebuilding and we will reopen there later in 2021. Until then, our home is at La Mama Courthouse on Drummond Street Carlton. For rebuild details see https://lamama.com.au/rebuild-la-mama/

During its 50 plus years, La Mama has presented nearly 2,500 shows, and we now average approximately 50 primary production seasons annually, as well as developments, seasonal La Mamica events (Musica, Poetica, Cabaretica and Cinematica), regular touring through our Mobile program, plus our Learning productions, play readings, and other special events. These will take place again in the rebuilt La Mama, and currently are presented at our second performance venue, the refurbished La Mama Courthouse, 349 Drummond Street. The box office and audience entry area of the Courthouse was short-listed in May 2018 for a Victorian Australian Institute of Architects Chapter Award.

An ever-increasing audience is drawn to La Mama productions, not only from the Carlton and Melbourne University environs, but from far and wide across the country.

La Mama continues to be an open, accessible space, actively breaking down barriers to the arts through programs, initiatives, affordable ticketing and a welcoming ethos that has developed over the past five decades. La Mama is home to many and open to all.

For details of all productions and events, and bookings visit:

www.lamama.com.au

www.ingramcontent.com/pod-product-compliance
Lightning Source LLC
Chambersburg PA
CBHW050025090426
42734CB00021B/3421